DATE

SAN FRANCISCO GIANTS

JODY BRANNON

CREATIVE EDUCATION

Nearly a century after the first Giants hurler took the mound, the great John "Count" Montefusco carried on the tradition in this 1979 double-header.

Library of Congress Cataloging in Publication Data

Brannon, Jody.
  San Francisco Giants.

  Summary: Follows the team's fortunes from 1883 to 1957, when it played in New York as the New York Giants, and through its San Francisco seasons from 1958 to the present.
  1. San Francisco Giants (Baseball team)—History—Juvenile literature. [1. San Francisco Giants (Baseball team)—History. 2. Baseball-History]
I. Title.
GV875.S34B7 1982b   796.357'64'0979461   82-16177
ISBN 0-87191-873-0

SAN FRANCISCO GIANTS

HOME OF THE GIANTS

San Francisco, Calif., is a city which sports the Golden Gate Bridge, cable cars, Fisherman's Wharf and one of the world's most fabled baseball teams—the Giants.

For over 25 years, loyal San Francisco Bay Area fans have braved dense fog and chilly ocean breezes to watch their Giants. Usually, by the time everyone settles into the seats at Candlestick Park, the bright sun burns through the mist. The spectators shed their jackets and soak up the warm California sun while shouting encouragement to their team.

They've cheered for San Francisco stars such as Willie Mays, Juan Marichal, Willie McCovey, Gary Matthews, Orlando Cepeda, Vida Blue, Johnny LeMaster and John Montefusco. These guys are only a handful of the great players who have proudly worn the Giants uniform. The all-time Giants roster reads like a roll call for the Hall of Fame. The Giants have been fielding feisty teams since 1876. Those early New York players began a winning tradition that Giants fans have come to expect ever since.

THE ORIGINAL 'NEW YORKS'

In 1883, a cigar-box manufacturer named John Day bought a baseball franchise. On May 1 of that year his New York team hosted a squad from Boston. General Ulysses S. Grant was in the stands, while two of the best pioneer ballplayers—William 'Buck' Ewing and John Montgomery Ward—were on the field for the New Yorks.

Juan Marichal swings from the heels in 1964 action. In 1982, the San Francisco fans selected Marichal as the greatest right-handed pitcher of the modern-day Giants.

MARICHAL'S STRANGE NO-HITTER
Juan Marichal, a control pitcher with a long wind-up and a high kick, had won five games in a row. But now he was going to be on the mound against Houston, a team which had touched him for several hits the past few outings. So, Marichal pitched the whole game using a shortened motion. He tossed a no-hitter that day in 1963.

7

New York won that home opener. Slowly the team developed into strong contenders. With players like Ewing, New York couldn't miss.

An all-around player whose face "seemed always on the verge of laughter," Ewing was called the best hitting and fielding catcher of the era. He was the only player in the nineteenth century to earn over $5,000 a year. He could bat lead-off or clean-up, and he was the first catcher to perfect the throw from a crouch.

In 1884, manager Jim Mutrie was so pleased by his team's powerful hitting and strong fielding that he shouted excitedly from the dugout: "My big fellows! My giants!" The New Yorks finally had a name.

Unfortunately, the Giants' success didn't continue during the 1890s. Mutrie retired in 1891, and the Giants went through 13 managers before a fiesty little Irishman named John McGraw finally took over the helm in 1902.

McGraw was only 28, but he was determined to revive the Giants and make baseball a more respected profession. He did. Soon, everyone wanted to play for McGraw, despite his hot temper and harsh manner. His players traveled in style. They rode in the best trains, stayed in the finest hotels and were the highest paid in the league.

TWO PITCHING LEGENDS

McGraw could have lured any player he wanted into a Giants uniform. But he didn't need any more. He had the best two pitchers in baseball at that time—maybe even of

The Irish legend. Feisty John McGraw skippered the New York Giants from 1902 to 1932, including four World Series in a row in the early 20's.

all time. Christy Mathewson and Iron Joe McGinnity were almost unbeatable on the mound.

Joe McGinnity was an underhanded pitcher with a sharply breaking curveball. His arm was seemingly made of iron. Three times during August, 1903, he hurled complete doubleheaders, winning all six games. Iron Joe had become a Giant a few years earlier when a scout told manager John McCoskey about a young pitcher who had struck out 22 females. McCoskey had a weak group of pitchers at the time. "Sign him up," he laughed. "You think one of my guys could strike out 22 girls?"

McGinnity went on to a 35-8 record in 1904.

McGraw had visions of a Giant dynasty. He knew he had a fine pitcher in McGinnity, and he saw the same qualities in Mathewson.

From the beginning, Matty was his pet project. Horace Fogel, the Giants manager before McGraw, had Christy pegged as a first baseman. After all, Fogel reasoned, he's big, strong and a steady fielder. Then McGraw arrived and said, "That's the dumbest thing I ever heard of. Mathewson has the most natural pitching motion I've ever seen."

He was right. Soon, the manager and star pitcher became fast friends. The Mathewsons even lived with the McGraws— the manager paid the heating bills and the rent while the hurler bought the groceries.

As a pitcher, Christy was such an immediate winner that a New York sportswriter quickly tagged him "Big Six," which meant the same as "the best." He was named after New York City's swiftest, most reliable fire engine company.

Old Reliable. This early batter was better-known for his awesome pitching. Christy Mathewson won more games in his career than any other pitcher in history, past or present.

MIGHTY MATHEWSON During the 1905 World Series, Christy Mathewson was unbeatable. He pitched 27 scoreless innings, earning three of the four Giant victories. Two spectators were discussing his remarkable performance after the third game, a 9-0 win which gave the Giants a 2-1 Series edge. "Matty was off form today," said one man. "Yeah," agreed another. "He walked a man!"

The shy Mathewson, a handsome man with unruly blonde hair and clear, battleship gray eyes, modestly said his nickname simply sprung from his being a six-footer.

But he definitely was "Old Reliable." Between 1903 and 1905, he won at least 30 games a season. If his legendary fadeaway pitch was off, his breaking curve took over.

In 1904, the Giants won the pennant, but a disagreement among the leagues cancelled the World Series. The 1905 World Series was all Matty's. Within six days, he shut out the Phillies three times to lead New York to its first modern-day baseball title. He pitched 27 scoreless innings, struck out 18 and walked only one batter.

In 1908 he started 56 games—more than one-third of the season—and racked up a 37-11 record. He was billed by the press as a perfect man, "a Greek god in flannels." Christy didn't smoke, drink or gamble—he didn't like cards and wouldn't pitch on Sundays. He'd rather challenge nine people at once to a game of checkers or chess while wearing a blindfold!

The Giants visited the Series in 1911 but lost to Philadelphia, four games to two. They lost to the Yankees in 1912 in the same grand contest despite the early season tear of another Giant fireballer, Rube Marquard, who won his first 19 games.

Matty had another super year in 1913. Between June 19 and July 18, he hurled 68 consecutive innings—almost eight complete games—without granting a base on balls. During the entire season, he walked only 21 of the 1,195 men he faced!

Manager Frank Robinson — the former outfield great — led the Giants into the 1980's with a dream, a plan and a smile.

Again Mathewson sparked the Giants into the Series. He won Game No. 2 for his fifth career Series victory. During that fall classic he worked 19 innings, allowed only three runs and had a 1.32 ERA.

Matty was traded to the Reds in 1916 and he turned Cincinnati into contenders. As a player, Mathewson had 373 career wins. Between 1903 and 1915 he won at least 20 games and on four occasions won over 30. Christy won more games than any other pitcher ever—more than Bob Grove and Dizzy Dean combined, more than Dazzy Vance and Carl Hubbel together. He still leads all National League pitchers with over 2,500 strike outs. A member of the Hall of Fame, Mathewson's plaque simply states: "Matty was master of them all."

Despite the heroics of Mathewson and several other Giants, McGraw knew as early as 1913 that he needed to rebuild the core of his unit with younger players. He got to work right away.

THE DYNASTY OF THE EARLY 1920's

By 1921 McGraw's machine was terrorizing the National League. That year the Giants made their first of four straight trips to the World Series.

Frankie Frisch was a Giants hero in each Series. Always a steady performer, Frisch sparkled in October. He was the first man to bat at least .300 in four straight Series. In 1921 at age 22, he hit .300 against the Yanks and set a record for most putouts in a Series by a third baseman.

Future Hall-of-Famers? Juan Marichal and Gaylord Perry limbered up for a 1965 contest at Shea Stadium in New York. Perry picked up his 300th win 17 years later — in 1982!

HALL-OF-FAMERS
At the Baseball Hall of Fame the Giants have a section set aside for San Francisco players who have thrown no-hitters. Juan Marichal, Gaylord Perry, Ed Halicki and John Montefusco are honored there.

In the 1921 Series, the Giants didn't score a run until they were behind 4-0 in the third game. But Frisch's bat ignited his team to a come-from-behind 5-3 Series victory over the Yankees, the last of the best-of-nine championships.

The following year, the same teams met again and the Giants outslugged the Bronx Bombers once more. Even the Yankees' legendary Babe Ruth managed only 2 hits, batting a meek .118. As for McGraw's boys, Heinie Groh used his strange bottle-shaped bat to hit .474, followed by Frisch (.471), Ross Youngs (.375) and Frank Snyder (.333) for a combined team batting average of .309. Blistering hitting!

Some people say the 1923 World Series results should be recorded in the history books to read like this: New York Yankees, four games; the Giants' Casey Stengel, two games. The Giants failed to win their third straight world championship, but Stengel's heroics kept the contest close. In one game he swatted a looping airball which cleared the fence for a game-winning homer. In another, he stretched a hit into an inside-the-park homer for the winning run.

In 1924 the Giants faced a new Series foe—the Washington Senators. The Series stretched to seven games. With the score tied in the twelfth inning, the tension was unbearable. Suddenly, the Senators' Earl McNeeley hit a routine hard-hopper to the steady Freddie Lindstrom at third. But the ball hit a pebble and bounced over Lindstrom's head. Washington used that break to score the winning run!

That final game marked the end of McGraw's winning era. In June, 1932, McGraw turned over the reigns to Bill

A rare photo of the great Casey Stengel, the hero of the unforgettable 1923 World Series.

Terry, a man whom McGraw had coached and groomed carefully to take over his team.

McGraw had been with the Giants for 30 years. He had won 10 pennants, including four in a row, and he had directed the Giants to three world championships. If you count the three flags won by McGraw's apprentice, Bill Terry, McGraw played a part in winning 13 of the Giants' 16 20th-century National League pennants.

TERRY TAKES OVER

Terry proved to be as good a manager as he had been a player. As a hard-hitting Giant infielder, Terry had become the last National League hitter to bat over .400 when he managed a .401 mark in 1930. His career average was .314—higher than Honus Wagner, Joe DiMaggio or Napoleon Lajoie. The 1930 MVP had also led the league in assists and put-outs for five seasons.

In his first full season as skipper, Terry directed the club from the cellar to the 1932 pennant—the first of three flags in five years. Part of his success was employing himself in the field. He served as player/manager between 1932 and 1936. Following the example of McGraw, he proved to be a wise field general. He, too, had an instinct for using the right player at the right time.

Of course, players like screwball artist Carl Hubbell made Terry's job much easier. Hubbell was always the right choice to send to the mound. Carl's nickname was "Meal Ticket." During those dreary days of the depression, a meal ticket

First baseman Bill Terry looked mighty fine at 1932 spring training. Later that year, he took over as manager and led the Giants to three pennant victories.

BEFORE THE WORLD SERIES... The Giants of the 1890s weren't a very good team, but in 1894 they finished second. In those early days of pro baseball, the top two teams would meet in a special contest, similar to today's World Series, to determine the world champ. It was called the Temple Cup Series and that year the Giants beat the Baltimore Orioles to become one of the few teams ever to win the Cup.

THE SCREWBALL GOT 'EM ALL

Carl Hubbell was really smoking on the mound during the 1934 All-Star game. He used only his awesome screwball to retire five American League stars in a row, each of whom are now members of the Hall of Fame. Hubbell fanned Babe Ruth, Lou Gehrig, Jimmy Foxx, Al Simmons and Joe Cronin.

was like money in the bank—just as Hubbell was a sure thing to pitch a great game.

Like so many other great players, Hubbell had originally become a Giant because of John McGraw's ability to recognize great talent.

In 1928, McGraw had heard about a young screwball pitcher who was knocking everyone back to the dugout. Naturally, McGraw sent his best scout out to see this young ace.

"They say that screwball he pitches will ruin his arm," reported the scout, "and he won't be any good in another year or so."

"If that's all that's wrong with him," McGraw replied, "buy him. Matty had a screwball — they called it a fadeaway in those days — and he lasted pretty good."

As it turned out, McGraw's hunch about Hubbell was a great one. During one period which stretched between the 1936 and 1937 seasons, Hubbell won 24 consecutive games, completing 19 of them. He allowed only 159 hits in 207 innings, walking only 39 men. In 19 appearances he gave up three runs or less!

Hubbell's 1933 ERA was a low 1.66, and he hurled the Giants into two World Series victories, as New York embarrassed the Senators, four games to one.

The following year, the Dodgers barely edged the Giants for the flag. In 1934 New York fell to third place, but in 1938 they were winners once again. Early in the season, the Giants were in fifth place, 11 games out of first. Then manager Terry took charge. On one July afternoon, he

Old "Long Pants" makes his 1939 debut. Here's Carl Hubbell, star Giants left-hander, breezing one through against the Cubs.

placed himself in the line-up despite his broken finger and sore legs. Boldly, he tore the splint from his finger and hobbled out to the diamond. He singled, doubled and tripled that day. After that, the Giants won 15 straight games and 21 of the next 22. New York claimed the pennant and earned the right to meet the awesome Yanks in the world championship battle.

Hubbell won the first game handily. In the second game, four Giant hurlers were shelled for 18 runs — every Yankee made a hit and scored a run. The Series was tied.

The turning point of the competition was Game Three — a real heartbreaker. Fred Fitzsimmons, the Giants' steady moundsman, held the Yanks to two hits. Unfortunately, one was a Lou Gehrig homer. In the eighth inning the score was knotted at one. The American League champs had a man on second and third when the batter hit a screamer back to Fitz. Fitz was the best fielding pitcher in the game, but this time he only got a piece of the ball. It glanced off his glove, a run scored. The Giants lost 2-1. The Yankees went on to win the title in six games.

During Terry's reign, tiny Mel Ott developed into a Giant superstar. At 5-9, 170, Ott was probably the smallest home run threat ever to play the game. He came to the Giants in 1925 — shy and scared and carrying a straw suitcase. He was only 16 when he stepped up to the plate (before the watchful eye of McGraw) to take some batting practice.

"Why do you raise your leg as you start to swing?" asked McGraw of Ott's funny habit of lifting his right foot during his cut.

Mel Ott, one of the smallest home-run threats to ever play the game, terrorized the league for the Giants until World War II.

THE GREAT OTT
Mel Ott is the only modern-day baseball player to score six runs in two separate nine-inning games. Several have done it on one occasion, but Ott's the only one to have achieved that in two different contests.

23

"I always hit that way, Mr. McGraw. I guess it just comes natural to me."

"Then keep right on hitting that way. Don't let anybody change you," said McGraw, for he had noticed that the young man never moved his head or upper body during his swing. In fact, McGraw didn't want anyone fiddling with the boy's strange batting style. Under McGraw's direction, the kid from Louisiana never spent a day in the minors.

The year Ott turned 20 he hit .328 with 42 homers. During the 1933 World Series he nailed the Senators' Walter Steward for a two-run homer that one reporter said "would be a home run in any park in America — including Yellowstone."

Even though players like Hubbell and Ott continued to play strong baseball for the Giants, New York fell out of the pennant picture in 1937 and were never really a threat again until after World War II.

THE 1950's START WITH A BANG

The year 1951 was an awesome one for New York. The Giants were 13½ games behind the front-running Dodgers on August 11, but at the end of the regular season, the teams had identical records. A playoff for the pennant was necessary.

The Giants won the first of the best-of-three series. Brooklyn forced a final game by winning the second.

In the third game, most people thought Brooklyn had

Another Giants big-stick. Outfielder Gary Matthews took Rookie of the Year honors in 1973.

sewed up the pennant. Going into the bottom of the ninth, the Dodgers led 4-1.

The first two Giants singled. Then Monte Irving (the hottest batter in the Series) popped out. Next, Whitey Lockman doubled in a run, and the score was 4-2 with men on second and third, one out. Bobby Thomson seemed nervous in the batter's box. He took the first pitch for a strike. When the next pitch came, he swung and connected.

"It's gonna be . . . I believe . . . the Giants win the pennant . . . the Giants win the pennant . . . the Giants win the pennant . . . the Giants win the pennant . . . Bobby hit it into the lower deck of the left-field stands . . . the Giants win the pennant and they're going crazy . . . I don't believe it . . . I don't believe it . . . I will not believe it . . . Bobby Thomson hit a line-drive into the lower deck of the left-field stands and the place is going crazy . . . and they're picking up Bobby Thomson and carrying him off the field . . . the Giants win the pennant . . ."

Those were the unforgettable words of Giants announcer Russ Hodges who would get so excited while broadcasting the games that he'd have to take tranquilizers to stop from yelling into the microphone.

Now Thomson was a hero. "Bobby toured the bases, leaping like an antelope. Before he had crossed the plate," wrote John Durant, a noted baseball historian, "ticker tape was streaming down from Wall Street windows and Giants rooters the country over were dancing in the streets."

Again the Giants were to face the Yankees, their crosstown rivals, in the World Series. The Yanks, who had won

THE GIANT WHO WORE THE FIRST BATTING HELMET Cincinnati's Andy Coakley beaned Roger Bresnahan so hard his skull almost caved in. He lay unmoving in the dust, his pulse very faint. Many people feared he was near death. But a month later, Roger returned to the lineup—as the first player to wear a batting helmet.

The Giants win the pennant! Here's Bobby Thompson hitting his famous home run in the Polo Grounds against the Brooklyn Dodgers in the 1951 play-off game.

27

three of the last four championships, had defeated the Giants in the Series of 1923, 1936 and 1937. The Giants had a score to settle, and they set out to do so with a vengeance.

The Giants won the opener, 5-1. It was the first time since 1936 that the Yanks had lost the first game of a Series.

Monte Irvin sparked the Giants in the first three games to give his team the series edge, 2-1. In the first game he had three singles and a triple. In the second he got three more singles and a double. During the entire Series, he had 11 hits in 24 at-bats for a .458 average. But his efforts weren't quite enough to carry the Giants. The Yankees took their 14th World Crown in a six-game series.

WILLIE MAYS COMES TO TOWN

Although the Giants were disappointed in the World Series, 1951 had brought them one grand prize. A young outfielder named Willie Mays was brought up from the Minneapolis farm club after hitting a scorching .477. The young star was so loved in Minnesota that Giants owner Horace Stoneham had to place ads in the newspapers, apologizing and explaining why he needed Willie in New York City.

"He showed up at the Polo Grounds with six bats, a shaving kit and a toothbrush and ... the biggest grin in Manhattan," recalled Hodges. "I'll never forget his pre-game workout. Of course he was facing batting-practice pitching, but he belted it all over the place. He whistled line drives to all fields and smashed screaming wallops into the upper

Stealing home! Giants outfielder Monte Irvin was awesome against the Yanks in 1951 World Series. Here, he beats catcher Yogi Berra to the plate.

deck of the left- and centerfield stands. Then he went to the outfield where he cut loose with that marvelous arm, winging the ball from deep in center to third base and to the plate without a hop."

After watching Mays' pre-game heroics, Stoneham hollered to Manager Leo Durocher: "Hey, Leo! How do you like him?"

"I'll marry him," grinned Leo.

Somehow, Mays got off to a slow start during his first few days in the majors. He got very depressed and even told Durocher maybe he'd better go back to Minneapolis. But Leo said, "Don't worry, Willie. If you go 0 for 50, you're still my centerfielder. You're the greatest and don't forget it."

Indeed he was the greatest.

The "Say Hey Kid" came out of his brief slump and became the 1951 Rookie of the Year. He served in the Army in 1952 and 1953, but he returned in 1954 to run up 41 homers, 110 RBI and a .354 batting average, a performance which earned him the MVP award. At 23, he was the youngest to ever receive that honor up to that time.

Willie led the Giants in the 1954 World Series against the Cleveland Indians—the American League champs who had won an amazing 111 games.

It was during this Series that Mays made one of the most memorable catches in baseball history. With the score tied, Mays made a spectacular over-the-shoulder catch of a Vic Wertz blast, grabbing the ball just before the warning track. The Kid saved a sure run with that nab. In the last of the ninth, the Giants Dusty Rhodes sent a Bob Lemon pitch out

The "Say Hey Kid". Willie Mays was Rookie of the Year in 1951, and played brilliantly for the Giants for 22 years.

MAYS BLASTS FOUR HOMERS On April 29, 1961, Willie Mays hammered four homers over the fence in Milwaukee's County Stadium. Each blast carried well over 400 feet.

of the park for a three-run homer. A pinch hitter, Rhodes was the Series hero. He had two hits and two homers in six at bats to drive in seven runs. He led the Series sweep for the Giants who became the 1954 World Champs. They were the first National League team to sweep the Series since the 1914 Braves.

HOW THE GIANTS MOVED TO SAN FRANCISCO

The Giants fell into third place the next year and finished in sixth position in 1956 and 1957. During these disappointing years, many of the old Giants fans stopped coming to the Polo Grounds. Rumors began to spread that New York just wasn't big enough for three teams (Giants, Dodgers, Yanks).

First the Dodgers decided to move out West. The Giants followed their lead, so the famous Giants/Dodgers cross-town feud could continue as a California rivalry.

Beginning in 1958 the Giants of New York would become the Giants of San Francisco. It was a town that loved baseball and dearly wanted a major league team of its own.

New Yorkers screamed and demanded the team stay. They made speeches, wrote to newspaper editors and called their congressmen. They demanded in the names of old Giants greats like McGraw, Mathewson, Stengel, Ott and Hubble that the team stay put. But they still didn't come to the stadium in large enough numbers to root for the team.

On the next to last game of the season only 2,768 fans watched the Giants/Pirates game. But at the season finale, nearly 12,000 came to say good-bye. Some tears flowed.

Manager Leo Durocher had a lot to smile about as the Giants stormed into the decade of the 50's.

34

Many of the old-timers who had proudly worn the New York colors were there for a special farewell ceremony.

The game itself was a disaster—the Giants lost 9-1. The real action occurred after the game. With the final out, thousands of spectators tumbled onto the field to grab a souvenir of the Giants' colorful history. The crowd fought over pieces of the bases. They ripped up the canopies which hung over the bullpens. Telephones were yanked out. The rubber padding on the outfield walls was torn off. People filled bottles with genuine Polo Ground dirt. The crowd chanted "Stay, team, stay!" during the entire destruction of the Giants home of 46 years.

Meanwhile, the players were in the clubhouse quietly packing up their equipment for the move out West to the land of orange groves and sunshine.

During the winter before the Giants debut in San Francisco, over $1 million was raised in season ticket sales.

Manager Bill Rigney held a press conference in 1958 to officially introduce Willie Mays to the local reporters. Everyone in New York had loved Mays, and Rigney wanted the people of San Francisco to do the same.

"Willie Mays is the world's greatest athlete," he began. "His motions are so smooth I even get a kick out of the silky way he puts on his coat. He is the only man known who can win a game for you in every department of the game, except pitching. They talk about his impossible catches. In 1957, we were leading Pittsburgh by a couple runs in the late innings and the Pirates loaded the bases. Roberto

THE RECORD SMASHER Willie Mays was a Giant for almost 22 seasons. During his Giant career he hit over 40 homers six times and hammered over 50 twice. He collected 3,187 hits and 646 four-baggers. All are marks that will stand in the Giants' record book for a long, long time.

In 1958 the Giants of New York became the Giants of San Francisco. Between celebrations, manager Bill Rigney took a moment to pose with the great Willie Mays.

Johnny Mize
knew that since
the second World
War was ending,
he would be back
in a Giants
uniform in 1946.
But at age 33 he
weighed a chubby
250 and he knew
he had to lose
weight. He
performed
hundreds of
calisthenics a day
in a zipped-up
tent on the
tropical Pacific
Islands. It was like
working out in an
oven, but he
arrived at spring
training able to fit
into the same
uniform he'd worn
10 years earlier as
a rookie.

Clemente smashed one that should have been a triple. No other centerfielder in the National League could have gotten that ball, I'll swear, but we know Willie. We watched him start the chase to his right. We waited for him to punch the glove—his instinctive signal that he's got it. We waited some more. It was a tremendous wallop and I groaned. But hold it! To this minute I don't know how, but Willie got there except he didn't have time or room to put out his gloved hand. Know what he did? He reached up with his bare hand and clutched it for the out. After that stunner to retire the side, Willie trotted to the dugout where he placed the ball in my hand. He smiled just a little bit, from the corners, and he said, 'Here's something for you, Skipper.'"

Willie had a strong season that first year in California, but San Francisco's first hero was a rookie named Orlando Cepeda. He hit .312, was named Rookie of the Year and was voted Most Valuable Giant by a newspaper survey.

The Giants finished third in 1958, but Giants fever was spreading all over Northern California. One survey said that over 70 percent of all the radios in the Bay Area were tuned into the 1959 opener.

In 1959, the Giants farm system produced another Rookie of the Year award winner. Willie McCovey had two triples and two singles in his first game for the Giants. San Francisco won six of the first seven games he played in. He collected five singles, two doubles, three triples and three homers. Even though he played only half the season, he won the best rookie award easily.

Willie snares one against the left-center field wall in 1958 action against the Cubs. Nobody robbed a batter better than Mays.

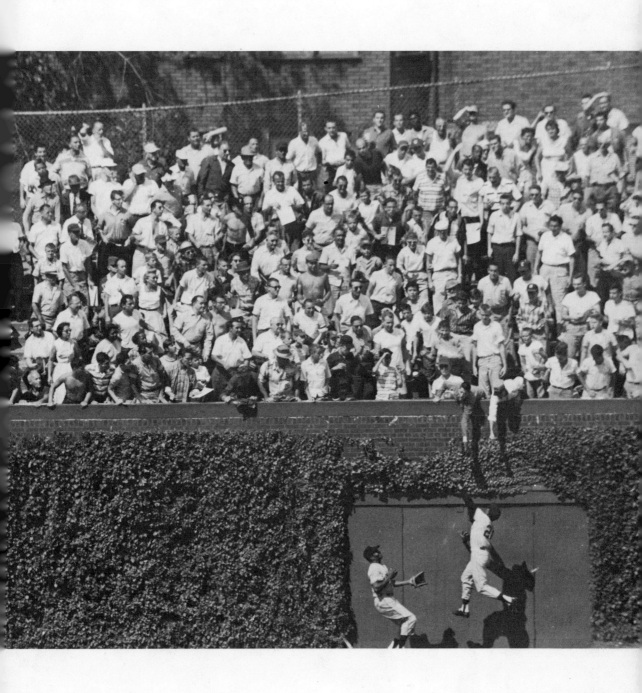

SAN FRANCISCO GETS ITS FIRST PENNANT

With stars like Mays, Cepeda and McCovey, San Franciscans were optimistic about their team becoming a real contender. In 1962, they got their wish.

The Giants had a poor pre-season but on opening day, everything came together. Second year pitcher Juan Marichal shut out the Braves' Warren Spahn, 6-0. Mays connected for his first of 40 regular-season four-baggers. The Giants were off.

In past years, the Giants had a tendency to fall out of the pennant race early. But not this year.

San Francisco was four games behind the Dodgers with 13 games to go, but manager Alvin Dark, in his second year at the Giants helm, wasn't worried. "The race will go down to the last day. We aren't through."

He was right.

The Giants won seven in a row, and they caught Los Angeles because the Dodgers fell apart.

"The Dodgers died at their own hands," explained sportswriter Art Rosenbaum. "Tired of looking back at the tenacious Giants whose playing seemed almost carefree, and a little frightening, too, the Dodgers stopped hitting, kept losing and were caught on closing day."

The California foes were headed to a three-game playoff. Dark again predicted the future. "We'll win it now, and we'll take the Yankees to seven games in the World Series."

The special play-off was almost a repeat of the exciting 1951 New York/Brooklyn squeaker which the Giants had

Three sluggers from the San Francisco Giants get ready to do damage in 1961. Orlando Cepeda (left), Willie Mays and burly Harvey Kuenn.

THE DECATHLETE WHO BECAME A GIANT
Jim Thorpe was a 1912 Olympic decathlon and pentathlon champ —the best all-around athlete in the world. But Thorpe was not just a track star. He played in the Giants' outfield for six seasons. His speed on the basepaths and in the outfield won several games for New York during his pro baseball career.

won on Bobby Thomson's ninth-inning homer.

Giants top of the ninth. The scoreboard showed the Dodgers leading, 4-2. A single, a force, a walk, a walk and the bases were loaded. Willie Mays was up. Willie slapped a hard slider back to pitcher Ed Roebuck who deflected it. A run scored. Bases still loaded.

Orlando Cepeda was in the box, and he had been in a slump. The Giants fans groaned. They remembered how Cepeda had popped out in the first, hit into a double play with bases loaded in the third and left a run stranded in the seventh by hitting into a force.

Stan Williams replaced Roebuck on the mound, but Cepeda hammered a sacrifice fly deep into right to drive in a run. The score was tied.

The bases were loaded again after a wild pitch and a walk. Shortstop Jose Pagan nailed another Dodger hurler for a hard grounder which Larry Burright kicked for an error.

"The Dodgers, leading 4-2, had been pressed into four walks, one wild pitch, two deflections, one that was scored an official error and both could have been outs, and four big runs," reported Rosenbaum.

The Giants retired the Dodgers easily in the last of the ninth and were crowned the National League champs. They headed home to Candlestick to meet their age-old rivals, the New York Yankees.

Just as Dark had predicted, the Series stretched to seven games.

First Baseman Orlando Cepeda is one second away from picking off Pirate Gino Cimoli in 1960 double-header.

San Francisco had the statistical edge in most categories: better pitching, more hits, more runs, more doubles, more triples, more homers. Still, in the bottom of the ninth, the Giants were one out away from losing to the Yanks again.

Now, Series hero Willie McCovey was up. Throughout the championship, McCovey had shown what a complete player he truly was. He started the second and fifth games at first base, the third in rightfield and the final game in left. He hadn't made any errors; he had smashed a homer in the second game to lead the Giants to a 2-0 victory.

The entire city of San Francisco and each of his teammates knew McCovey could win the game for the Giants. He took a mighty swing at the next pitch and the ball sailed away— right to a waiting outfielder.

If McCovey had hit the ball just an inch more toward right, it surely would have been a homer. "No human can hit a ball harder. Nor with lousier luck," sighed a disheartened sportswriter.

But the crowd of nearly 44,000 was very proud of its team. The Giants had given San Francisco its first pennant in a thrilling unforgettable season. San Francisco was a city of champions.

TODAY'S GIANTS

Each year since their 1962 World Series appearance, the Giants have struggled valiantly to win another pennant. Only once since the divisional play-off system began in 1969 have they actually won the Western Conference title.

Grand-slam king. First baseman Willie McCovey donned a big grin as the new leader in career grand slams. (1977)

MVPs
Over the years, five Giants have won the National League MVP award. They are: Larry Doyle (1912); Bill Terry (1930); Carl Hubbell (1933 and 1936); Willie Mays (1954 and 1965); and Willie McCovey (1969).

After the Giants captured the 1962 pennant from the Dodgers, the Giants flew back to San Francisco. Over 100,000 people were at the airport to greet their heroes. But the police couldn't keep the hoards off the airstrip. The plane was forced to circle the airport and wait for the people to move back.

In 1971 they lost to the Pirates in the National League play-offs, but they came right back in the years to follow, struggling to capture their old magic.

During those years several super players proudly wore the brilliant black and orange of the Giants.

Mike McCormick won the Cy Young Award in 1967. McCovey was the 1969 Most Valuable Player.

Willie Mays played brilliantly for the Giants for 22 years before he was finally traded to the New York Mets in 1972 so he could finish his career in the city where it began. At the end of the 1981 season, Mays still held 13 team records.

Bobby Bonds roamed the Giants outfield from 1968 to 1974, and set the all-time San Francisco record for scoring 134 runs in a single season.

Hard-hitting outfielder Gary Matthews was named Rookie of the Year in 1973. Pitcher John "The Count" Montefusco won the award in 1975, winning 15 and striking out 215.

Johnny LeMaster came up through the Giants' productive minor-league system to become their starting shortstop a few years later. LeMaster became the 43rd player in the majors to hit a homer in his first big-league at bat when he nailed the Dodgers' Don Sutton for an inside-the-park home run in 1975.

The list of Giants honors and achievements goes on and on, growing deeper and more impressive with each new season.

Today, Frank Robinson, a former outfield flash with the Reds and Orioles, is at the helm, anxious to lead the Giants

Big Mike McCormick mowed 'em down in 1968, easily taking the Cy Young Award as big-league baseball's finest hurler.

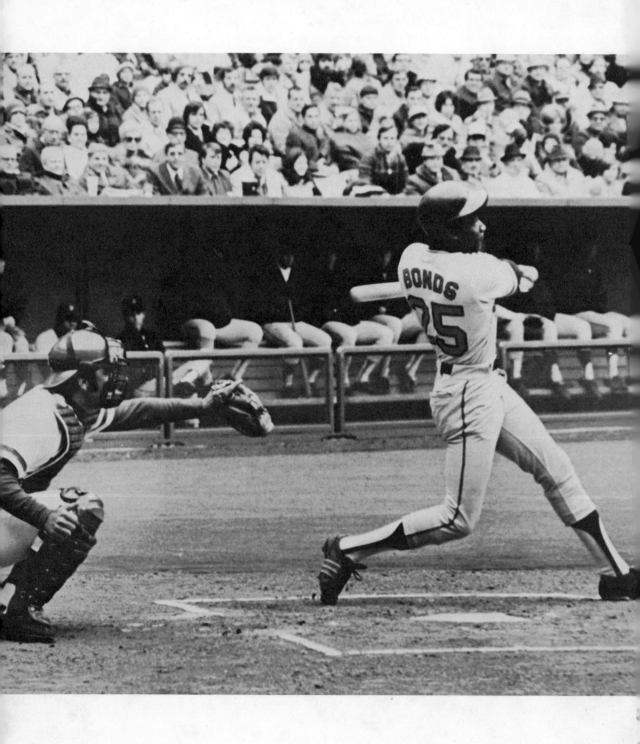

back into the pennant races. In his first year as skipper, Robinson directed the 1981 Giants to a winning season — their best since 1973.

Today's San Francisco Giants team is a young one with plenty of talent, determination and energy. Outside of San Francisco the players' names are not very famous—yet.

Just like the 1962 pennant winner, today's squad brings heart-stopping excitement to the city by the Bay. The fans know there will be many more winning seasons for San Francisco. It's simply a matter of time before the pennant waves from the pole above the bleachers in Candlestick Park. Meanwhile the loyal fans are still in their seats, warming themselves in the bright San Francisco sunshine.

In 1982, the Giants celebrated their 25th anniversary in San Francisco. In honor of the many great players who have served the city, a "San Francisco Dream Team" was selected. The stars named to the team were: Tom Haller, catcher; Willie McCovey, first; Tito Fuentes, second; Jim Davenport, third; Johnnie LeMaster, shortstop; Gary Matthews, leftfield; Willie Mays, center; Jack Clark, right; Orlando Cepeda, infield/outfield; Juan Marichal, right-handed pitcher; Vida Blue, left-handed pitcher; Stu Miller, right-handed relief pitcher; Al Holland, left-handed relief pitcher; and Frank Robinson, manager.

Giants all!

Somehow, Bobby Bonds would get on base and score. He set an all-time San Francisco record for most tallies in a single season — 134!

THE GREAT RIVALRY
In the 25 years that the Giants and Dodgers have played on the West Coast, the two arch rivals have traded players to each other only once. On Feb. 13, 1968, the Giants sent Tom Haller to Los Angeles for Ron Hunt and Nate Oliver. In 1986, Candy Maldanodo came to the Giants in a trade for catcher Alex Trevino.

The modern-day Giants are led by spirited guys like Johnnie LeMaster, the cannon-armed infielder who never says die.